MASTER *your* EMOTIONS

Copyright © 2022 by Queen Phoenix

All rights reserved. No part of this book may be reproduced, stored in or introduced in any forms of photocopying, transmitted or recorded, without consent from the author.

ISBN 978-0-578-25667-2

Printed in the United States of America
Collierville TN

This is a work of fiction. All characters and incidents are of the author's imagination.

liveinlove1111.com

This book is dedicated to all my soulmates, my twin flame, my false twin and my karmics. I love you N*****

A special dedication to one of my soulmates George Vassell from Kingston, Jamaica. Its because of you this book is born. Thank you for touching my heart in the past life and coming back to touch it again.

Special acknowledgements to my loved ones who left the planet before me.

To my niece Tishekie Lane. You set the bar high, boy did you ever. I still use you as the Perfect Example.

Aunt Joanne Stridiron. Boy do I ever miss you. Can we go out and dance all night? Can you talk that real shit to me? Can we take that trip to St Thomas now? Damn! Can you call me in the middle of the night and curse me out one last time? I love you too Auntie.

My cousin Ebony Godley AKA Loiuse. Little did you know, you were just as dope as your mother. I had an epiphany that you were a blessing. Can we have one more Thelma & Louise night? See you in the astral plane.

Daddy Leroy, you are still the true King. Signed, your only girl.

Dear Mama, can you come back. I know that you are whole now. Can you hug me this time? Can we talk? I am so blessed to have been your daughter.

Acknowledgements

Thank you to everyone I know because even the ones I thought were hurting me was really helping me. I needed and gained from every energy that I have encountered. Nothing is personal, only vibrational.

I don't have many special thanks for being there for me or being an extraordinary blessing or going the extra mile for me. Just Spirit every time.

My daughter Queena Dowdell who had become my best friend. You were right there during these trying times. Through my mental break downs, fears and my tears. You were a relentless listener when I was confused trying to figure it all out and you supported all my big, crazy wild ideas. Your energy and presence of beauty grounded me during times I thought I wasn't going to make it. You taught me to not judge and that I could support you through ANYTHING.

To Kierra Payne, thanks for listening!

To Shaleka AKA MoFire who blesses me with that Aries energy and its real and vibrant every time.

To my children Willy, Jaquey, Queen, Kareem and Kai. It's been a journey. I am EXTREMELY proud of ALL of you. If given another chance, I would choose all of you again.

Willy keeps me intellectually challenged

Kareem keeps me spiritually evolving

Quey keeps me brave

Kai keeps me young

And Queena keeps me grounded. I love you ALL unconditionally.

Table of Contents

Acknowledgements v

Chapter 1   George 1

Chapter 2   Wounds Cause Emotions . . . 13

Chapter 3   Projecting Emotions 17

Chapter 4   Kids Feel Too 23

Chapter 5   Intimate Emotions 30

Chapter 6   The Truth 36

Chapter 7   Judgement 72

Afterword 77

You want to know how to master your emotions, let me help you with that. Let me give it to you raw, uncut with no chaser. I have been there so I can relate. I'm real. Emotions are real. So let me keep it real with you. It's not about, not getting angry, upset, pissed the fuck off, sad, depressed or jealous. You don't pretend as if you're not feeling it. That's not real. That's fake and in order to fix anything you must keep it real. And let's be real, we have all felt like shit, bombarded with unwanted emotions. And don't be like my brother. My big, little brother. He be like, "That's me, I got angry issues. That's just me. I can't help it. I get mad." I kick that real wisdom to him. That shit he get for free and everybody else pay for. But he try to talk that foolish shit to me and I raise my voice and have to overpower him. Cause he big, little bro. "No mother fucker, that's not just you. You choose to be like that. You were not born with that temperament. That's anger.

It comes from somewhere. That's energy that needs to be released. It needs to be channeled. Anger is sadness that have not been addressed. So, you have short patience. One uncomfortable situation triggers all the built-up unaddressed issues. You explode easily because of the stuck energy. Remember, energy is never destroyed, only transferred. It has to go someplace. It must be released. You must channel it." I start making sense to him and he listens. Then he gets it. He respects me on the low. "Oh, I see what you're saying. That makes a lot of sense."

I started my journey to mastering my emotions when I did not see my three-year-old son in six months. My favorite, my love child, my soulmate, my crystal baby born during a high vibration. I had to breathe and do many things because I wanted to pull up on his father who felt like he had reasons to take my baby, and like I was that type and for that one I had it in me to take his life and everybody helping him. But the love for my son was much stronger than that. I knew that those actions would surely cost me my son. I wouldn't be able to raise or love him properly from a jail cell. And I loved him enough to spare his father, even though he had betrayed us both. I began suppressing my feelings. I shoved them deep down inside to avoid feeling them. When his name was mentioned, I conveniently changed the topic. I told my loved ones that I did not want to talk about him. I pretended as if I did not see his pictures. I became a tea kettle. Steam started to rush out of the top. I lost control. I hyperventilated. My body shook out of control, and I couldn't think straight. I had to find ways to cope. I had to convince myself that I wasn't dying. And that I would be alright, and my son was alright without seeing my face and hearing my voice. That our love was so strong that he could still feel and remember it and that he was not going to forget me. I had hoped he didn't feel abandoned. And that he knew what was really going on. Because facts were, he was older than me and his father by vibration. I had to trust in my spirit guides that there was a plan. I had to remember that the good and bad work together for the greater good. Everything happens for a reason. There are no accidents. And for that, I had to master my emotions.

CHAPTER 1

George

For three years I had built myself up by healing inner wounds and loving myself. I learned that love come from inside and you cannot get it from nowhere else and that you can only share it with someone. I know that to be true because I now have it. So, when I met George and we went into physical and spiritual sync from the first meeting of eyes I lost my sight. Right away he told me that he liked me and if I wanted him that he was mines. It was hard for me to trust him after that. It was hard to choose a man that was willing to jump in the waters not knowing how deep it was. He didn't know me. I expected him to get to know if I was worth his time and love. But no, he wanted to commit the first day. There was something about him that stop me from totally turning him down besides his caramel skin and his tightly structured face with the high cheek bones he inherited from the Indian in his blood. His hair was longer than mines with an Indian texture. His eyes were lethargic and drunken, and they penetrated every part of me but mostly my soul. His Caribbean accent was the cream cheese icing on the cake. Even though on the surface I saw a low vibrational being I was connecting with his soul. He had been on Facebook posting his pictures with a scripture saying where my single ladies at. I wondered what was a handsome man doing searching for a woman in such a way. He explained to me that he was forty-six, getting older and was ready to love someone for himself. I don't know how we made it to the next day. I was looking for a man who came across like he had it together. Knew about the matrix, herbs, self-love and was a bit cautious. George was free. I saw loneliness and lack of self-love and self-esteem. But maybe he just knew what he wanted. I remember knowing what I had wanted in no time before. After all were all energy right. Even though I was cautious and suspicious every day got better. Peace and joy came over me. A calmness came over me and I didn't know it. I remember him telling me that he felt so much peace since he met me, and I noticed it on him. He was so happy, and I didn't trust it. I judged him for being lonely. Truth is I might have been lonely too, just not letting it all hang out the way he did. It's funny because three days leading up to when we met, I was anxious and out of sorts. Almost as if I felt something coming. I didn't know what it was all I knew was my body felt sensational and my soul was pulling or being pulled. My eyes were all over the place. I just didn't know what was happening to me. And because I was following principle, my ego and societies norms and not my heart I still didn't see it when he showed up. Those three days it felt like I was running around Grand Central station, running for a train with very little time and I had made it. Maybe George was on that train. Lucky for me the train was still there. We would face time all night while he was in his bed, and I was at work. My soul was content the entire time. I was dating a Jamaican man who lived in Kingston Jamaica. He was consistent with me and unbelievably loving and sweet. He reached out to me every morning before he went to work and whenever he reached home. Anytime I spoke with him all he did was recite romantic words over and over again. He always told me how beautiful I was over and over. He told me that he wanted to love me forever. That he would make me happy and not disappoint me. He was always missing me and grateful for me. And all I thought about was how? when he didn't know me. I kept thinking he would cheat on me. It was hard for me to believe that that type of love for me was real. Why didn't I believe him? In my three years of celibacy, I found out how dope I am. I started loving me and really liking myself. He had every reason to be in love with me, "shit," I was in love with me. Deep down I knew that he was genuinely crazy about me. Like set for life winning ticket crazy. I was Brownan. A light skinned woman was considered a prize to the Jamaican man. Plus, the soul doesn't lie. We glazed into each other's eyes, and it was a standstill. He could talk and I would just stare into his eyes while listening to him. I was calm, happy and content. He loved my calm aura and said I was a good listener. But he was a good lover. I was scared, so I told him that I couldn't date him anymore. It was the weirdest thing. It was almost as if I didn't love myself. Because "what the fuck." He had sent me a video called never knew love like this by Stephanie Mills. I had sent him treat me by Cashma. That's how he made me feel. I wanted to send him stardust by Haley Smalls. He was so hurt because he tried to make sense of it and couldn't. He tried to check up on me to see if I was okay but I gave him a hard time and so he sent me one last message. It said, "ok bye," and he blocked me. I just shook my head and let it go because I was used to saying no thank you to men. I was looking for perfection with my Virgo ass. Plus, I knew enough betrayal and if that fine ass mother fucker hurt me the edge was going to tip.

After a week I noticed that I had George on my mind more than I would have liked. I was missing his smile, the admiration towards me, the way he looked at me, the way he looked into my eyes, his consistency, his un hesitation to tell me he appreciated and wanted me even if he seemed desperate and lonely. There was some purity in how he felt for me. I felt it too even if I was taking my precautions. I was confused. I battled the heart and the mind, "shit!" It was a fucked-up feeling. Damn! I said while I asked the spirit what to do. I noticed that there were no clear messages coming through. I felt like I should let go and I wanted to because he blocked me and that was too damn immature for me. Mind you, I knew what I wanted, and it was a whole man. Someone who could communicate, problem solve, master his emotions. How could I go back to someone who couldn't handle an issue? How could I even consider a man who couldn't communicate to the point he let it all go. He spoke an extreme amount of romance words but no sense. I could trust practicality. I need practicality. For those reasons he is not my man. I told myself that he was desperate and lonely. I paused and looked to the ceiling. Who am I kidding, so am I. The difference was he was real about it, and I wasn't. Well, the feeling is human, so that's okay but we need to be aware of it and have some type of self-control. "Spirit, I'm confused," One thing I do know is that he is from my past life. He is a soul mate. I have the experience to know soulmates. I also knew that soulmates came to teach us lessons and not necessarily meant to stay. Just because we didn't go through a dragged-out relationship just to get the experience and lesson did not mean he was not my soulmate. It just meant that I was highly vibrational enough to get the lesson sooner than later. I felt like the lesson was listen to my intuition. George was teaching me to listen to my intuition. It would be the perfect time to learn that and to take my intuition seriously. I was evolving so much spiritually. Spirit was taking me to a level that depended on my intuition more than anything. I needed to believe in my powers and my guides guidance. I kept going back and forth. Why should I call him or go to Kingston to see him even as a friend? He is the man, and he has not made any effort to reach out to me. Well, he does have the right to feel like I am not interested, after all he does feel like that. And I am the one who cut him off. He has the right to feel some way about it. What about his emotions? Who am I to assume that he is lying? Isn't that control? Yes, and it is fear. Fear that I am not good enough. Fear that he will leave me for someone else or that he would cheat on me. That's why it was so important for him to be practical and not so much romantic. Because I could see bullshit on the ground but not in the air. Basically, my heart was guarded. I was scared. FEAR! I hate that bitch. Who is that bitch? I know of him but never seen the mother fucker. All I know is that I hate that mother fucker. He might be the reason I'm alone right now. Who introduced me to him? I hate that mother fucker too. My heart began to beat outside my chest. I suddenly knew who George was. I had an epiphany. It told me to write. I grabbed my pen and paper right there at work. The Line by DVSN played over and over in my head. I could feel George singing it to me.

This is what I know. Love should be free and should not come with conditions. We cannot contain love. It cannot go in a box and stay. We can't stop people from feeling something for someone and we should not get jealous when someone we love do. We should accept love from everyone that love us and enjoy them while we can. This does not mean fall in love or lust with someone, give all your goods to them, have sex with them and put all type of expectations on them and hate them when they don't live up to them. You can simply explore their world and appreciate what they are giving you. Don't fear what you are feeling. You can do this by trusting your intuition. What is love? Love is accepting humans. You must understand humans to accept them. This is what makes compassion a love thing. Not someone touching you between the sheets on your private parts that react because of your biological make up. You will realize that sex has nothing to do with this after that tower moment when it all goes crumbling down and realize that you cannot control anyone and what you seek is control. Love is free. Save yourself heartache and love everyone. The trick is love yourself first. You will never allow anyone to mishandle you. You will never give away all your stuff in exchange for what you think is love. When you can apply all of what I just said, you will attract love and guess what? It will stay. Be love!

So, what would I tell Phoenix? You know I am not one hundred percent sure. But my first level of understanding would be to go with the flow. In the meantime, take it one day at a time. Feel what you are feeling and get an understanding of it, have compassion for it. If the opportunity presents itself to communicate with George again be totally honest with yourself and him. Try your best to just allow him to be himself without judgements. This is love. This way you will get to know him, and he will feel free to be himself while you are exploring his world. Then you can decide what it is you want to do, and this will depend on how you two meet in the middle or wherever you meet at. Just remember none of this is possible with fear and without trusting yourself. Continue to date but don't chase. Love people, explore people, understand people and accept people but do not put expectations on people. If the shoe fit, then you can wear it. If the coat looks nice to you and it is also warm enough for your temperature, I'm sure you will enjoy wearing it. What I have told you was a way to master your emotions when in so called love or lust. Whatever you want to call it. In order to succeed at it you must master self-control, discipline, realization and always consciousness. Its okay to feel things such as jealousy, betrayed, worthless, low self esteem and anger. This is great. Know that it comes from a place, and it will not help you in any relationships. It is also important to know that those emotions did not come from your mate even if it seems that way. They are only helping you acknowledge them. You have to find the root to these emotions. It will be coming from a past experience such as past affiliations. Our parents have the most impact. Prior relationship traumas can impact us the same. You must heal from every emotion that causes insecurities and play out in your behavior and affect your relationships. Feel that emotion, sit with it, talk to it, understand it, have compassion for it then transcend it. This is power. This is evolution. This will help you master your emotions. Remember emotional mastery is so very important, it is connected to your peace and your love.

CHAPTER 2

Wounds Cause Emotions

Many times emotions come from wounds. I had this thing about being different. I knew things that I could not explain how I knew it because I just knew things. How? Because I'm claircognizant, I'm empath. I have Jupiter and mercury in my twelfth house, so I'm intellectually connected to the divine. Messages come straight from the heavens. A blessing and a gift, you would think, and I thought until my parents and all the adults around me who didn't share the same vibration told me that I didn't know and that I should not say things or think things because I could not prove it or because they didn't have my gift to read energy. So, guess what happened. I was conditioned to not trust my intuition. To not trust myself. And you know what else? I lost my voice. Expressing yourself and having emotions was a form of disrespect. So, as a result I grew up not knowing how to manage my emotion. Shit! I didn't know what they were. Most of us were not taught or allowed to feel or embrace our emotions. So, there I was, African decent, woman in the corporate America, in the matrix struggling. I didn't talk white and didn't like white talk. On top of that I did not know how to express myself the way I needed to. I was different indeed. I knew energy. I spoke the truth that no one accepted. I am a rebel so if I had to yell or knock someone the fuck out that's what I did to get my point across. How does that work in the professional world? It doesn't and it didn't. I worked as a registered nurse. I busted my ass to get that position only to not want it anymore. I don't want anything to do with corporate, in fact I'm too holistic and real to pretend like I'm helping someone under big pharma's instructions and guidelines. I don't need that type of karma.

Wounds Cause Emotions

Today I teach individuality because I use to be uncomfortable being the me no one accepted. I was triggered when I spoke, and I wasn't taking seriously. I couldn't get my point across. People didn't believe me, and I couldn't talk right. I stuttered and I got angry. I couldn't control my emotions, so I cussed people out, manipulated them and tried to control them. All because no one would listen to me. They thought I was crazy just like everybody else did when I was growing up and it bothered me. Guess what happened when I healed after pinpointing the wound. I don't force my spill. I say it with confidence and humility. If one is not ready to receive, I let it go. My favorite word is "OK." And I mean it. Silence is white gold and I prefer it. I'm not forcing shit. I don't even care that much. When someone is ready, they will come, and they will receive. Sometimes I listen to people talk stupid and I don't say anything. When they are done, I walk away without a response. Its funny to most people and it is if you think about it. But I am serious. I put my words in the book now. I make more of a difference and more money that can buy my freedom. I pay for people to leave me the fuck alone. That's what everybody like and want from this material world. I be like here take this money and leave me the fuck alone. And they do. If I paid the taxes on my land for a hundred years, they would have no reason to knock on my door or take my houses and cabins away. Yeah, free America is not so free. You noticed that? I would like to know who sold America or Mama Earth to them. Why is it that we are paying them? I want to know. But, whatever.

CHAPTER 3

Projecting Emotions

What happens when people try to project their emotions onto you? Typical, annoying shit. But you have to step away from the ego. Acknowledge it. Know that what is happening and taking place at that very moment is a fucking illusion and guess what? You don't have to buy into it. When you master your emotions know that you don't have to react to others behavior, to others ignorance, to what they don't know and have not mastered yet and you can respond instead. Don't react, respond! Respond in such a way that they will have no choice but to receive. All this is possible when we understand. Understand humans and energy. Understand what you are dealing with. And most importantly, understand yourself. That's how we can accept people. You learn and you know that other being's actions have nothing to do with yours. It's a reflection of what dwells within them. For their lack of knowledge and wisdom, their insecurities and fears. IT NEED NOT AFFECT OR BOTHER YOU! Therefore, you need not feed into it. Often, we feel offended, and we call it the principle. "Who the fuck they think they talking to like that?" But the real question is, who are you to care, and why do you care? It's because you feel a certain way by the way you look when the people around see or hear. You feel like a punk or fool. Deep down inside there is some belief to what that person has said to you. True or not, you believe it or else you wouldn't care enough to react. You feel foolish when people talk to you with base or with authority because there is a reason why you don't like no one telling you what to do. Maybe you have a self-worth issue, and you think people could see your flaws. When someone speaks to me with base and attitude I respond on a lower, normal, natural tone because its not that serious. I acknowledge the hype and ADHD, insecure energy and I pity it. Let's say I understand it. They have not reached that level of maturity and humility. I will respond with an. "ok." And still get my point across on a level that they can undersand. They need to feel superior. It's fine with me because I win at the end because I killed their ego with my kindness. They now feel in control, and they begin to like me. They begin to respect me. It's not that they like me, it's I am no longer a threat. It did not cost a thing.

Just like at the workplace. Emotions tend to get lost there. I am a RN, I supervise. I work evening and night shifts only. This is because I don't want to be around the big wigs. They do too much. I'm not with corporate. I can't be controlled. I won't be micromanaged. I am well aware that they play a bigger part with the responsibility of the ship. And I get that but sometimes they wigs be too tight. You put me in position to lead then let me do my thing. If I fuck up, check me, correct me. I respect that.

My emotions are managed. As far as my part at the workplace, I use my stellium in Aries at all times. The emperor. I'm assertive. I take initiative. I don't back down, just lead. I check myself first. When I come to the floor, sometimes I smile and sometimes I don't. But my energy is always humble, professional, treating every situation accordingly. Number one rule is respect. I give it and I get it, never having to demand it. I look you in your eyes and say it. I treat everyone like human adults. I don't micromanage. I say hi before I speak to you, whether I care for you or not. I ask the questions I need nicely, but not passively. I ask is everything alright, I check my surroundings and if everything copasetic, I say "ok" and I leave the unit. On to the next. I sit in my office and do my own thing. When they call me, like the sheriff I show up. In any situation I delegate while doing my part. Our ship moves smooth. I know my shit and I do my shit. I don't play around with people, and I don't gossip. Yes, emotions get projected onto me but its theirs not mines, I'm unbothered. I don't care enough. Only my kids move my spirit and I'm

Projecting Emotions

working on that too. Sometimes I have to tell people to punch out. But I allow people to speak their minds. I don't feel like just because I'm the Captain, the General that everyone else must kiss my ass. All that means is I'm responsible for the moving ship. You must learn how to lead. As long as my ship is moving, its all good with me. At the end of the shift all the asses on my ship are covered.

But that's just me and you wont always be fortunate enough to work on my ship. And guess what? I know what its really like in that corporate America. And you know that I can't stand it. Today, I get in where I fit in. If I can't be myself, "I can't service here," and you won't catch me there. Money don't scare me. I know how to make it. I would never put a Covid concoction in this body. My point is, if you are working somewhere that you are unhappy, you will have a hard time managing your emotions. When I speak with the big wigs, I'm unwavering. They can't play with my emotions. I don't care how light their skin complexion is, how narcissistic they are or how high their position is. I'm not afraid to hear them say "Your fired." I would just say, "you got it." Working is in addition to my multiple streams of income. People, you must get independent. Because if you are dependent on this matrix, they will control your emotions. Don't think that you are independent because you have a crib, pay your own rent and buy your own food so you don't need no one. You do need someone. You need that job, and you are dependent on that position. You are only free to work.

CHAPTER 4

Kids Feel Too

It is very important for you as an adult to learn to master your emotions so that you can teach your children how to manage their emotions. This way they can become healthy adults, mind, body and soul without having to unlearn false teachings and having to heal from wounds that you project onto them. Otherwise, they will manage their emotions the same way you do yours. In my generation most urban parents raised their children to stay out of grown folk's face. We could not join in grown folk's conversations. Speaking your mind, not agreeing or having a different view from your parents meant you were talking back. If we cried when we were hurt or felt violated it was, "You wanna cry? Let me give you something to cry for."

If we can't join in grown folk's conversations how else do we learn to communicate without feeling inferior to authority. If we can't speak our mind, disagree, or express our own view how else do we learn to debate and disagree without feeling offended. How do we believe in ourselves enough to stand up for ourselves? If we can't cry how else do we learn to manage our emotions. Is this why we shove our emotions deep inside and explode later. Caucasian kids would say "I hate you mom," and stomp all the way to their room and slam their door. The Caucasian mom would keep her cool naturally and even empathize with Johnny. She would knock on the door. "Johnny, can I come in? Johnny never answers. Mom walks in. "Johnny are you okay?" "Go away mom!" "Oh Johnny, I'm so sorry you feel that way. I love you." Then she takes the time to explain principle with him and show him the bright side. At the end they would hug. Is this why Johnny goes out in the world feeling confident and loved, like he is somebody and he matters. He learns about his emotions, and he gains self-esteem and self-worth because his mom loves him unconditionally. Not just when he is good. When mom knocks on Johnny's door, he learns the importance of boundaries and privacy. There is no need to be controlling. Try telling a black mother you hate her. She will try to break all the bones in your body, put you down and cuss you out. "Mother fucker, I brought you into this world, I will take you out." "Who the fuck you talking to like that?" "Oh, you slamming doors." That's another ass whooping. Knock on the door? Yea right. "This my mother fucking house. I pay the bills in here.

I'm not saying Daquan was right. I'm not saying he was wrong either. He is dealing with emotions and mom needs to help him. Mom is definitely wrong. What she did was physically abused him. She put her hands on him as if he was not a King. She taught him to deal with his emotions with violent behavior and foul language, instead of teaching him how to use his words. She taught him that just because she pays bills, she is in control. It's no wonder Daquan snuffed Deandre over a petty quarrel. This is why when one express how they feel to another, that person refuses to receive it and it is taking as offense instead. Because that man mother straight violated him for expressing his. He don't know how to talk it out with you. He feels like if you don't have something good to say, don't say anything at all.

Ladies, you let your daughters watch you change boyfriends like your draws. Because you can't figure out what's wrong with you and why you can't keep a man. You haven't figured out that you are controlling and lack self-love. You chase behind dudes that sell drugs and don't have a place of residency of his own. Your daughters listen to you argue with your boyfriends about cheating and not meeting your standards and then you lay down with them. What is this teaching your daughters? I don't have to tell you. They grow up and repeat the same shit. Because they do what we do, not what we say. Remember?

Action speaks louder than words. Let's not do this. Let's teach our Queens how to be Queens by creating a stable, clean and calm environment. So that they don't become a drama queen in their homes. Let them watch you chase dreams, not people. Show them how to set boundaries by not allowing anyone to use you. Do not bring drug dealers in your home. They are watching and this is the type of men they will choose because it has been normalized in their home. We have to talk with our kids like they exist. Let's love our kids by doing more than providing. If you don't, they will grow up to be providers only. Then they will tell their children they are good parents because they kept a roof over their head and never starved them. We haven't figured it out that that's not enough. Do you know what happens when they don't get hugs and you don't tell them that you love them and that you are proud of them? They will give their money or their bodies in exchange for love, then assume that something is wrong with them when they don't get it. They will also seek validation from others because they haven't figured out that they are good enough. They will lack the ability to understand their emotions. This is where we are today. I know you heard the term generational curse, right? That's what that is. Let's break them. "These kids these days are something else!" Shut up! No, they are not. You just haven't figured out that you are. Our kids are not disrespectful, they are free. This is the generation of freedom. So, they are rebels. They seem rebellious without a cause because they refuse to conform to this matrix. They are being raised by parents whose parents were raised as slaves. That is where all those rules come from. This is why our parents beat us to keep us in check. Because that's what happened with the slaves. This is how they prepared us for this matrix. And look around, it worked. Our children are mirroring us, trying to teach us that we are wrong. When we bully our children, we are making them weak. Then they go out in the world and fall in line. They go out there feeling inferior. Look at the black man and the white man. For some reason the Caucasian just seem ten times more confident than the kid from the projects. Can we stop this. Who cares how we was raised? They were right but they were wrong. That was then and this is now. It is a whole new world. Let's hug these boys and girls up. Treat them like Kings and Queens. Let's talk with them like they are our friends and build a bond. They will be stronger. Remember when they told us you can't be your kid's friends. That was a control tactic. So that it would be clear who had the power. Fear me or love me. Love is the answer. You shouldn't be friends with your kids. Think about that. Does that sound right? Why not? What is the meaning of a friend? Friends trust each other. They tell each other everything, share secrets and be there for you. And don't say that a friend will also cross you. That was never your friend. Queen Phoenix is telling you that it is okay to be your child friend. It's healthy. Friends have influence, right? No more cussing or yelling, okay? Now! If you can do all of what I have just told you, your children will master their emotions.

CHAPTER 5

Intimate Emotions

You ever sit down with your lips twisted, arms crossed and just pissed the fuck off after kicking your mate out or you're the mate walking down the street after getting kicked out and you have no clue what the fuck went wrong. Let me tell you.

Whole people know how to communicate. They use their words. "Baby, can I talk with you about something?" She or he say it with respect and humility and it's a question. Not, "I need to talk to you," with the evil eye and the negative body language. You have already cursed the conversation. The other person will have trouble understanding you because he or she is now trying to understand your negative body language and building up a defense towards it. They cant hear you. Your problem is, you can't communicate, your whole purpose is control and to make that person a slave to what you are lacking. Love. The love you're looking for is unreasonable. You want him to love you the way daddy didn't. The problem is he can't because he is not your daddy, and you are not a little girl anymore. Grow up! When grown woman look for daddy love, it looks like this, "Why didn't you call me, what took you so long to call back, where you going, where you at? They want you up on them twenty-four seven. They will ignore their kids. Mama and child both trying to get the same thing. You too men. Who is taking care of your kids while you laying up under Shaquana's ass? These females be like, "You don't love me." "You don't touch me or spend time anymore." Yeah because you getting old. Let that man go outside. He could be doing his best and you will never know it. He can't fill your void because he is not daddy. You think if he doesn't put you before himself that he does not love you. Its's quite the opposite. If he put you before he puts himself, then he does not love his self and then he can't possibly love you. He can submit to you temporarily to get whatever it is he feels he needs and that's it. If he was to grow up like a boy is supposed to, he wouldn't want you because only a girl would allow what you do. He will leave you.

And ladies don't ask me, "What about these no-good ass cheating men?" And tell me that that aint right. I know that it is not. But riddle me this. Why are you still with him? Just don't tell me love. He has the same damn problems you do. Relationships are healthy when two people are whole. When broken people come together it gets chaotic, in other words toxic. This is when you see his and her emotions. This is what you call little boy and little girl syndrome. Just like kids. You ever see two broken people go back and forth. They look like kids, right? Whiney, angry, pouting and sometimes they throw things. They both want something and mad about it, like, "me, me, me." Words are in the air just up there crossing. Nothing is being received. That's why old stuff you thought was squashed already come out. You two are just beefing until someone says let's stop, I love you, I'm tired or hungry, you look cute when you're mad. Then he or she smile, she cutting a eye because she know you full of shit but she going to take the make up sex, food and Netflix because that feels better and that's what you both really want. Meanwhile nothing got resolved. You know what's wrong right? The problem is deeper than that. You both need to heal. If you cannot heal while together then you will live out a toxic, unfulfilled relationship that result in lack. You forfeit your life purpose. You can't step into your higher self and become the best version of you. You two will resent each other in the end. Or it eventually comes to an end even after twenty years. Why do some of you think time matters. "Oh, we been together a long time already." So! Just because you have been going the wrong way for so long, doesn't mean keep going nowhere. "Or we have history." Right! And that's just what it is. Do you care at all about your future? When you two finally separate take time for yourself. Do not jump into another relationship. Use this time to heal. Reflect back on the relationship. What part did you play in it? What were your emotions? Figure out where they come from. Why is it so hard to let that man be a man? Why are you so insecure, jealous? Why are you lazy? Why are you angry? Why? You can ask yourself. The answer will appear. You just have to be ready for it. Be real with yourself. Practice on family members by being around the difficult ones. Love them, get along and if you can't, find out why. You have to treat your partner like a man or woman, not your child. But you must be one also.

Without boundaries you open the door for people to come in and trample all over you. You end up resenting them and other emotions show up like anger, and depression. Then feelings of not being good enough sneak in. Now these emotions must be understood and released. If not, that energy will build up like bags of trash that becomes weight, which is a load too much to bare. Then instead of loving people, you create walls to keep them out. Because you can't trust yourself to trust your intuition. It's a vicious cycle that robs you of your joy, love and life purpose. To stay healthy, we must be conscious, make better decisions and in ritual, consistently release unwanted festering emotions. We do this by addressing anything that does not feel right and manage it with understanding and maturity.

CHAPTER 6

The Truth

What if you have to, "What they call it?" Tell somebody off, also known as put them in their place. I'm not going to lie. I have humility. I can maintain my temperament. I appreciate humans and it is my specialty to understand them. But one thing about me is I speak my truth. No one will ever change that. I speak when necessary and never to hurt anyone. Granted, there are situations when not many words are needed. I can allow a human to believe whatever he or she wants. But there are instances where what you have to say must be said and it won't be liked. My voice does rise sometimes, I make faces and my actions will let you know that I mean what the fuck I say, and I'm not scared. What I'm saying is I'm not afraid to say what I'm saying. I say it and I say it straight. I don't stutter and no one talks over me. I'm classy and my words are effective. You know why? I don't say things out of emotions that I cannot control. I don't speak from an angry place. The spirit speaks. I just channel. If you feel or look like you got shut down, the spirit shut you down. Let me give you an example. My brothers girl friend texted me one day and this is what it read: Idk what the fuck is going on or what I ever did to you that bad that you would even come out your mouth and tell people in ya family that idek like that I'm a coke head and I smoke you was phoney kicking it and talking behind my back when I was at ya house too whatever you and ya brother go through ya'll go through don't involve or put my name in shit and as far he a crackhead naw he not you don't sleep with us or in this household to know what's really going on keep my name out ya mouth I don't dog ya name thru the mud don't do mine like that period misery loves company I see I'm out ya life you won't hear or see from me again it was nothing but love on my end hope all stay well with you tho.

"Gheesh," I thought. That was a lot. Although not enough to move my spirit. I had to first understand it. It took me by surprise. I was at work, sitting at my desk in the supervisor's office. I was being misunderstood and violated again. I had just been violated by my uncle the prior day. So, these humans were taking turns with me, playing with my emotions. But I was calm, just as I was with my uncle. This was wrong of her. I had no idea what she was talking about. Why? Because I had not said anything about her having a drug addiction to anybody. The bond that we had was better than that. I expected her to ask me, talk with me about what you heard. Instead, she wrote some fucked up shit as if I was that fucked up person. If she truly knew me, she would have known I'm not with gossip and I don't play kindergarten. I actually loved her. I do not like her for my brother, but I accepted her. I can master my emotions because if I couldn't she would have been lunch meat a long time ago about my brother. But I'm grown now, and you know what them grown folks say, "If he like it, I love it." They shit was so toxic I was better off not touching her or should I say hurting that girl because he couldn't leave her alone. He couldn't see the person he had become but I did, and I couldn't stand it. Not my big brother getting played like that. What can I do besides detach myself and let their karma play out. At the end of the message, it said clearly, this person is unavailable on messenger. In other words, she blocked me. Not enough love or respect for me, just emotions. I chuckled, shook my head and smiled. I wasn't talking to my brother, so this was convenient for her, I thought. "Oh no you don't." I said to myself, while I got ready to send my brother a text message so that she could get my comeback.

To Jaymie:

You send me a message and then block me from responding…we don't do those…you were better off asking me a question because I don't know what the fuck you talking about and at this point, frankly, I don't give a fuck…I would never call you a coke head because I don't see you as one, crackhead maybe but even that I never called you…and for the record whatever I say out my mouth are my words, I own them, so I say what the fuck I want…You could never control that… Same way you choose to offer my brother advice about me and Sunny and join in conversations you don't have any business in…as far as you being good to me, I was good to you as well… You could sleep with my brother all you want… that's all you gonna do…remember this…he will always be my brother, but will he always be your man? Don't worry I'll wait…as far as miserable, look in the fucking mirror at your self-inflicted toxic as life…So now go sit your emotional ass down somewhere…I wouldn't give a fuck if you never called me again…who the fuck are you Bitch…NOW! Whoever the fuck you talking to about me is a fucking liar…everybody is hating on me around this time, and I don't even give a fuck…If I said something about you, I will tell you straight…I am the realest they come…now

The Truth

you can block me. Then I threw my phone on the desk, sat back in my seat, smiled and said out loud, "Who's next." Did I sound mad? Because I definitely wasn't. She just had me thinking. I didn't want to think about it any longer, so I served her back her own energy. Let her deal with her own emotions. Don't give them shits to me. I was grateful. I like learning about people I keep close. Don't get me wrong there are some cases when I ignore people. It don't be worth the energy sometimes and most of the time people just don't get it. But she gets it and she needed to know, especially fucking with my brother. That prophet right there is my son and one of my soulmates. There was a time I would have laid down my life for him. If my fear factor worked for me, it didn't work when it came to him. I didn't know fear when it came to him. Because I would react for his safety and best interest and think later. But that kind of changed because over the years I learned that he never cared about my safety or well-being the same. He wasn't safe at all. In fact, often times he sacrificed me. Another reason why is because I know the truth and I know what to do with these emotions. I'm a wizard. What that make you to me.

My eleven-year-old son Kareem who played the biggest part helping break my generational curses. He was my biggest mirror. He would not allow me to behave like my family had for generations. He broke me down over and over until he broke open my heart chakra. It was bizarre because he came to Earth and meant business by willing to accept any condition of suffering by any means necessary to get the job done. I feel like crying just to comprehend that. This took years. I ran from myself for many years. After a while Spirit and Kareem got together and jumped me. Like, "now is time." This was my spiritual journey accelerated. Kareem put the mirror up close in my face and there was nowhere to run. I couldn't move. Me moving was like losing everything, including my baby. Kareem brought out the anger in me. He would go to school throw chairs, flip tables and refuse to follow suit. His behavior was so unpredictable he had a para, someone who stayed with him until school was out. He told me that he didn't like school. I had a well put together talk with him. He heard everything I poured out, he agreed to listen. I told him that he had to, and he didn't have a choice. He was threatened and punished. I exercised the maximum punishments. None of them worked. We were in the suburbs, they were not wit it. At all. Everyday, "I'm sorry but someone has to come get him." If no one did I was picking him up from Cpep or Upstate Emergency. Monday through Friday, no days off. His behavior at home was nothing like his behavior at school. But when his principal put pressure on me, I put pressure on Kareem. Shit got real bad when he began to deceive me. He had a tablet that he loved. I took it and locked it up in my file cabinet. He broke in it and was using it in his room, in the middle of the night. That was the fucked-up straw right there. That type of shit I couldn't accept. I applied pressure. I gave him the evil eye. I told him the truth about me and that was I'm not that one. I didn't tolerate shit like that. I didn't care who you were. I stood in his room talking crap. I let him know if he couldn't follow rules that he couldn't continue residing with the rest of us. I let him know, "Do it again and I will find a place for you." It didn't matter. He didn't change. I was convinced that I had to change. Me change? Let a kid win? Never! My heart was not designed like that. I was not raised like that. In fact, kids were nobody. My big bro and I did two bids together. Rikers Island was reception on Vanduzer in Parkhill, Staten Island NY. I was four years old, and he was six. Mother did her. Big bro and I were on our own while she ran the streets. I lost my virginity to rape as a result. Mama's guilt helped her take Daddy Leroy's offer who moved her to a house in West Brighton. It gave us stability. He also gave her more kids. Big bro and I lived in the room that we shared. More like the cage that we shared. From Rikers island to the upstate penitentiary. We did seven years together. From four and a half to twelve years old. We went to school and straight to our room. My brother was my cell mate. So, when people wonder why he and I are tighter than a virgin, that's why. Yes,

The Truth

I am my brother's keeper. And loyalty is who I am. We could not watch tv on school days or go outside. We could not come out the room. I read books all day and big bro wrote rhymes. Friday and Saturday were the only days we could watch tv and go outside. Because even prisoners get wreck. Mama stayed in her room and Daddy Leroy worked. Big bro and I did not get any adult interactions. No conversations, and no hugs. Adults didn't talk to kids unless they were correcting them. And we didn't get away with shit. Discipline and structure was big on Cary avenue. They beat the shit out of us. Poor behavior was despised and not tolerated. So now, I have a kid who wouldn't conform. And there wasn't anything I could do about it. I couldn't accept that. In fact, I couldn't bond with him because of it, because our parents hated us for poor behavior. That was the curse that Kareem broke. He showed me that kids do matter. He taught me how to love unconditionally, bad or not, accept me for who I am. Just because I accepted the no hugs, no respect, no acknowledgements, he wasn't going to. And

I had to figure it. Every time I asked the spirit what was wrong with Kareem with my lips turned up and pissed the fuck off. My intuition led me to love every time. I did not want to accept that. I knew that I ignored him. I knew that I did not hug him. I knew that his love language was affection, and that Pisces must be touched. Truth was I didn't know how. My mother never wrapped her arms around me. I can't even remember having a conversation with her. She had every reason to be proud of me. I was a straight A student, smart and lovable. Every day I had love to give in abundance. Daddy Leroy use to call me in his room to ask me how to spell words. I was elected to compete in spelling bees. I won more than once. Teachers called on me to read in class because I never faulted. But mama never told me that she was proud of me. After Mama died, I lived with her mother for a few months She was worst than my mother. She didn't talk to me even after losing my mother. On top of that she gave me looks that made me think that she didn't like me. She avoided me. I couldn't please her, and I wanted to. She took me to the nursing home with her to see her mother and guess what? She was worst than them both. Mean with capital letters is all I could say. You see where I'm going with this. The truth is I saw myself in Kareem. He was a lot like me when I was a kid. The odd one out. Weird. Not only did I not want to be bothered with him, but no one did. He was not accepted, just like I was not. We were too different, too smart, too analytical, too knowing, too psychic, too real and too free to be accepted. The difference was he was much stronger than I was as a kid. I conformed and was weak. I was afraid of my parents. I was a sucker for their love and still didn't get it. Kareem stood his ground in who he was, and he didn't ever have to say it. His actions said it all. Queena and I dropped him off at the crazy house he waved goodbye. Queena and I said no way was that real. When the crazy house didn't work Queena, and I dropped him off at a residential school where he would reside for a few months. He hugged us goodbye and asked us when we were coming to visit him as if we were his friends. When we incarnate for this human experience, we choose our parents, and we all play the part we suppose to play. That's why I'm not mad at my father. Unfortunately, I can't fuck with him because he still molesting people. Kareem was too much for me. I needed someone to help me or take him off my hands. I had tried everything. I even tried hugging him, here and there. I stopped ignoring him and allowed him to talk while I listened even if it was about space. Every question he asked I could never find the answers to. I was not use to that. Kareem still didn't change. I figured we were telepathically connected, and he knew that I could do better than that. Having relatives down south that take in extended family members and change their whole program was a beautiful thought. I use to see movies where kids spend time in the south and it changed their world. That is what I wanted for Kareem. I had an Uncle Rick that lived in Florida in a beautiful house with his Caucasian wife and no kids. He had crossed my mind several times but for many reasons I thought that analysis was out. I love all my kids, bad, good, indifferent, gay, cripple, I wouldn't give a fuck. I'm Mama Bear. My first move is to protect mines. Control my emotions? Fuck with THEM. I had always been overprotective over them. Yes, I wanted Kareem far away from me, but it mattered where he went. My intentions were never to throw him to the wolves. Love was my number one goal. And I did let him stay with someone who had that love for him, me, all my kids and her kids too. Love was something that she embodied. She had it. I wanted her to give that to my boy. I dropped him off over there and went back to get him a week later because her family curse was poverty and I saw what it did to her family. Love didn't save them. Love alone wont work. We need more than that and that is exactly what her son taught me because he loved my dirty draws, I think. And I wanted to stay but for other reasons I had to move on.

My uncle in Florida could have been the perfect solution because of his location and lifestyle. But it wasn't actually ideal to me because he was my mother's brother which means they were raised up the same and with the same two parents. Chances were, there would be no difference, or the situation would get worst. Uncle Rick was known to be tough. He spoke with base, and he was strict in general and with humans. He didn't take shorts. He told it like it was and if any of his sisters called, he was knocking you out first, asking questions last. He almost had every reason to be cocky. He had sex appeal just like the rest of his brothers and sisters. He was tall, yellow brown, with red tones and muscular built. If you ran into him in the streets, it was a guarantee you did a double look. He would surely outshine the crowd. Period. That went for all grandpa's kids. My cousin Antwan use to stay with him when he was young and all he can say was," Man that man is strict. You got ten minutes in his shower." I looked puzzled, like, "What!" as he told me the story. He was like." Yeah, I'm not lying. And he meant that shit too. I was in the shower, and he knocked on the door and said," 'your ten minutes is up. Come out or I'm coming in to get you. You don't need anymore time than that to wash a few parts.' "I thought he was playing so I kept washing up." Antwan was demonstrating himself in the shower. He was into it and so was I. "Yo! this nigga came in and said, lets go." Antwan and I busted out laughing. I pictured the scene. "Yo! After that, I called my pops like somebody got to come get me, send me a ticket or something. I got to get the fuck out of here A-sap." It was funny because if you knew grandpa, Uncle Ricks father, he was just like that. Grandpa was an Indian. At one point in life his hair made it to his ass. They said grandpa did a number on his nine boys and four girls. They were raised in the Bronx, New York. Grandpa use to pull his gun out in the house and shot fire. Auntie said whenever her friends called the house that he would say, "No she not here, she dead." Antwan had many more stories to tell that spelled out to me bootcamp. Uncle had one son who he didn't get to raise because his son didn't want any parts of him, said he was mean. He had two big dogs that he treated like his kids. He had a shed in the backyard furnished like a living space. It had heat and a futon, but it was still a shed. His dogs stayed in it and that's where you stayed if you were ever a visitor. You could not sleep in his house. After spending so many years in prison and had gotten older he seemed more easier to get along with. Instead of dissing people he tried to build relationships. He was close with my big bro. They had a relationship so whenever he called, and I was around he wanted to speak with me, but I was never as interested in him as he was with me. He even tried calling me a few times, but I didn't answer. He has done some things to me that was not real right with me. Certain things make more of a difference than others. I can tolerate my aunt and uncle robbing me, or even arguing then what Uncle Rick did. I remember two things. The first thing was he came by my apartment when I was around seventeen or eighteen years old to pick up my aunt, his sister to take her to Florida to stay with him. Auntie was going through things, she needed to sit down for a while. I remember him walking in my crib, not acknowledging me at all. He said, "Where she at?" Auntie popped out. He said, "Would you come on, I got to go. Where we going, they don't have houses that look like this." What he said played in my head until I just left it alone. But I never forgot that feeling, that shame, that low ball. He didn't know my struggle. I was lucky to have a place at that age, holding down myself without looking for help from anyone. It was his sister that didn't have a place and couldn't get her shit together. She was living with me, robbing me, getting high and bringing me the fuck down. But I loved her. My baby. The second thing he did was call grandma house, his mother while I was there. He asked to speak to me. When I got on the phone he asked me a personal question, my business. I answered in which I didn't have to. He called me a liar and told me to get off his mother's phone. This was a man who knew nothing about me and never gave me a chance as if I was not his sisters daughter. Now I am a grown overachiever. I have more houses than he do and their paid for. The family look up to me, speak highly of me and my account stay fat. He knows that my brother come to me and get racks at a time. Uncle Rick Capricorn ass love money. Now he wants to be nice to me. I believe its genuine now and I'm not mad. I don't feel a way. It's just my spirit is not interested. What can I say? And even after what he did to me I would still send my son to him to help make a difference. But all because of that generational curse, that was a no. There was times Kareem took me to the point where I was going to send him to Uncle's bootcamp. I asked one of my uncles that I was way more familiar with to ask Uncle Rick. And I was surprised that he said yes. I highly respected that. I appreciated him. No one else would help. I'm not a fast mover on certain shit so I never sent him. I kept trying ways to cope.

My mother and her brother Uncle Andre were close when she was alive. It just so happened that so were he and I. He would pop out on me and stay for a month. No one understood our vibe. But it wasn't like uncle and niece. It was more like brother and sister. I understood him and respected him. I gave him what he needed in a way no one could. And he did the same for me. He knew that I was hated on. But he respected my real. He was being transformed around me and that's all that mattered to him. He had served time in the army, and he wear his dog tag royally. He will tell you that he had an honorable discharge. I figured it was the army in him whenever he came over and whenever he seen something needed to get done, he did it. He got to everything. And whenever I pop out to Brooklyn, he would take me around his neighbors and brag about me like I was a celebrity. We had long talks and listened to all Peter Tosh's songs. Uncle Rick called his phone. "Who house you at?" "Put her on the phone." "Hey Uncle, what's up?" Uncle Rick got excited. "Listen, listen, I'm in a jam." He was trying to put words together to explain his situation, prove his credibility, and make himself seem like he aint no bum. Just in this hole. "I'm in this hole. But I'm going to get out. I got this plan. I just need this here and I'm going to pay it back in interest. I always pay my dues. Andre knows. I called this and that one and they said this and that. "How much you need Uncle." I had been waiting for him to just come out and ask. I was prepared to say yes.

I didn't need the long story. And I already knew that he was far from a bum. I was giving it to him because my account allows me to do that, and I didn't forget he had agreed to help me out with my son. "Niece I need two fifty, but I can pay back three fifty. He began to tell his story again. Fuck it, let him talk. I noticed that he liked to talk anyway. He came off as lonely to me. He was bored in Florida. He was always trying to get everyone to go down there. Show his house off and try to control people. Everybody called him controlling, had to be some truth to it. Uncle Andre and I was chilling anyway. Every night was vibrant. When Uncle Rick came up for air, I spoke up. "You want me to cashapp it to you?" "You know what niece; I don't have that but my wife do. She will be back in the morning. You can send it to her. "Before we hung up, he told me how much he really appreciated me. I was thinking like he did all that talking for some petty cash. Not even a rack he needed. I was prepared to lend him one of those the way he was talking. He started talking about covid about how God told him to take it. He sounded like he thought he was so fucking smart and that if he said something then that was what it was. He was nice and cocky. I just let him talk. "You should really get the covid shot niece." I didn't say anything at all. I couldn't wait to hang up. He wasn't as tough as he thought he was to me. He sounded real dumb talking about covid to me. After I sent that money, he would text me all day. Like we were suddenly best friends. I wasn't looking for that. I lent the money, but I wasn't worried about it. Like, "You good, fall back. I'm busy." But I tried. I love him. He is my uncle. I will give him the shot he never gave me. He texted me saying he had made some money he could pay me now but he needed to wait. I told him no, take all the time you need. I want you to get on your feet. I won't be going broke no time soon. I believe that you're going to pay me back. He kept trying to prove himself to me. I told him that I believed in him. We got close enough for me to ask and consider my son going with him. That day Uncle Andre and Queena had to chase Kareem down the street like they were trying to kidnap him. I needed him to go somewhere away from me. Uncle Rick said, "bring him." Uncle Rick face time me and spoke to Kareem as if he had broken his curses. He told Kareem he loved him. He asked him if he wanted to go to his house to stay. Kareem said yes. Uncle Rick told him that he had two dogs and a pool. "You like dogs?" Uncle Rick asked Kareem. "Yea," he said. Uncle Andre said, "Why you keep saying yea? Don't say yea. The word is yes." "Shut up Andre! Don't tell him what to say. Let him talk. If he wants to say yea he can," Uncle Rick said. And that's when I knew my son would be alright. Uncle Rick was happy. He told me that I was doing him a favor. He wanted a kid, any kid so that he could teach him everything he knows. He wanted to give back. He told all his co workers that he was getting his nephew. This made me happier. Uncle Rick wanted to do it. This would help all of us. He had no kids and he was sure to spoil Kareem. Uncle Rick was strict, so I was sure that he was going to use the reward system with him and that's what he needed because Kareem did right if it was something in it for him. Punishment didn't work for him. You had to pay him and that was a problem for me. I asked Uncle Rick what if Kareem behavior there is as bad as it is here. He kept saying, he is a good kid, he just needs a different environment, a man and more attention. But I want to know are you going to send him back if he start to act up with you? Because if so, there is no need to send him. "No, I'm going to work with him." I had drove Uncle Andre back to his home in Brooklyn. He was going to get on the Amtrak to take Kareem to Uncle Rick and he was going to stay down there for a week with them. I notarized paperwork for Uncle Rick, and I gave Uncle Andre five hundred dollars to give Uncle Rick so that if he wanted to get Kareem any clothes or whatever. The whole trip to Brooklyn Uncle Andre kept telling Kareem that he was going to meet his probation officer. But everybody was happy. I went home feeling relieved. I knew I needed to heal and get myself together. I was going to do my best with myself. When they reached Uncle Andre called me. "Yea, so guess what?" "What?" "So, we missed the train right. And I had to take like fifty-six dollars out of his money." "Oh, ok." I was wondering why he was telling me. He had to use it on the tickets, so what was the big deal. When I heard Uncle Rick in the background. They appeared to be on speaker phone. "Uncle Rick said, "Yea, niece tell him that he have to give that money back. He took that out of Kareem money." I agreed with him, but I had a bad feeling. Something inside me said that was not an inappropriate way to play that situation out. Why was he focused on replacing that money if it was used for his ticket anyway? I thought. Well maybe he just wanted more money to spend on Kareem and it was Uncle Andre fault for missing the train. I guess that means he should pay for it. I was suspicious of him to have those type of feelings. Queena and I were in the mall shopping when Kareem called. "Hi mom. This my phone number. Uncle Rick bought me a phone and a tablet. He said you have to pay him back though." I passed the phone to Queena. "Talk to your brother. Something felt wrong. While Uncle Rick was at work Uncle Andre and Kareem called me. "Mom Uncle Rick said that you didn't give him the money for the phone, and you owe him one hundred and seven dollars" I did not respond. Head full of thoughts, playing the situation out. "He said that he is going to take it back because you didn't give him the money and that you make more money than he does." I did not respond. I changed the subject instead. The next evening, I was laying in my bed taking a nap. I had an hour left before I had to get up for my night shift. Kareem called. "Hi mom." "Hey, what's going on son." "Oh, Uncle Rick said that I need a bike because I have to ride it to school. He said you have to buy it." "Kareem?" "Yes mommy." "How come he keep mentioning money to me when I gave him five hundred? How come he don't take it out of that?" "Hello. hello?" "Shit!" My phone had gone dead. I reached over and set it on my lamp that had a charger surface area. I went back to sleep. Queena woke me up at eleven thirty. "Oh shit!" I had overslept. I jumped up and threw on my uniform. I grabbed my phone and realized that it hadn't charged. I did not sit it on there properly. I ran quickly to the car and plugged my phone up with the car charger. I was speeding. Texts began to come through. The DON had texted me asking me where I. was There was a text from Uncle Rick. I scanned through it quickly and couldn't believe what I was reading. I was spooked. But it was real. The text read: I heard what you said about me I'm going to send you back your 500.00 and I never asked you for money, but you disrespected me Kareem will be back with Andre bye still love you but I'm not that person. And you wouldn't answer your phone but that's okay your son wanted to be with me. I did not know he was like that. There was nothing grown about that text. When I got to work, I called them. I made sure he heard the sleep in my voice. I told him that I had overslept, and my phone went dead and that I was just getting his message. I also told him that I was disappointed with his message. I was humble, understanding and alert. "I'm saying, you disrespected me." "How?" "You told your son that all I want was money from you. I never even asked you for any money." He said a mouthful. Mostly stupid shit. I listened. "Ok, let me tell you what happened. Kareem said that I needed to buy him a bike and I asked him why you were asking me when you could just use the money that I gave you." As I was explaining he cut me off." "Let me finish saying what I'm saying. I did not interrupt you, don't interrupt me. I made a big move sending my son down there and for you to say will send my son back that easy, that is something different." He kept saying I disrespected him. He wasn't getting it. "Why you keep saying that if I just explained to you what happened. He kept referring to Kareem as the kid. "Can you stop calling him the kid. His name is Kareem can you call him Kareem?" "I can do you one better; he is going back with Andre." "That's fine I said. "Goodnight." And I hung up. I was in a state of shock, but unbothered. It was expected. I was calm. I did not raise my voice or disrespect my uncle. I was only sharp. He was starting to sound a little slow to me. I was fine with the outcome. I was not mad at all. When I spoke with Uncle Andre the following day I never mentioned it. I didn't care enough. Two days later Kareem called me on speaker phone with both Uncles listening.

"Mom?" "Yes Kareem?" "Uncle Rick said that I can stay but you have to send money for me to eat and for a bike and stuff. And I want to stay. Can I mom?" I was quiet collecting thoughts. "Can I mom?" "I'm thinking Kareem, stop asking. I want to make sure I say this right." "Yea, make sure because your on-speaker phone," Uncle Rick said. "Oh, I'm not worried about that." Uncle Rick cleared his throat and said, "Yea, I told him he could stay, he wants to stay and I want him to stay. But you have to send money. I don't have any kids and its not fair to my wife, he is not her grandson. He eats a lot and shit. I can't afford to take care of him but he can stay, he is my nephew and I love him, "How much do I need to send you?" I asked. "I don't know," he said. This nigga is stupid I thought. How you going to say you don't know. What do you know besides that unnecessary base in your voice? In my mind I knew the answer was no. I just wanted to say my spill. I listened to him say he couldn't afford him and he was not his wife's grandson. It sounded real separated to me. He didn't need him if he couldn't afford him.

The Truth

I finally spoke. "Well, I think it would be a really good thing for him because of the environment and I think that you might be good for him, Although, I'm not really sure. I'm learning that I don't really know you like that. The thing is I made a very big move sending my son to you. There was a miscommunication, which is fine. Nothing is wrong with that. That happens. That's when two adults discuss the situation and get an understanding. But you threatened to send my son back, just like that without having a conversation with me concerns me. I am uncomfortable with that, so I have to say no. I don't think that is a good idea." "Yes, or no?" Uncle Rick asked again. "No. I can't do that," I said. Uncle was offended. "Ok, bye." He hung up. He wanted me to kiss his ass for Kareem to stay and it wasn't that serious to me. I didn't trust him. People shouldn't say things that they don't mean. Imagine what will happen later. That was my son. I don't play on those levels. I picked up the phone and called Uncle Andre's phone. "Uncle Andre let me speak to Kareem." "Phoenix? You don't want him to stay? I think he should stay." "I'm sure you do Uncle Andre, I pray for the day you get a backbone. Let me speak to Kareem." "Hey mommy." "Hey, take me off speaker." "Listen I know you want to stay and I want you to stay. But sometimes we make decisions that seem right at the time but it ends up not being right in the end." "You know what I'm saying?" "Yes." "Okay, you are going to come on back." "Put her on speaker phone," I heard Uncle Rick say. "But she told me to take her off," Kareem said. I could sense that I was on speaker anyway. "Uncle Rick?" "Yea, he answered. "Remember when you said I had disrespected you?" He said yes. "Well, now you're disrespecting me. I am talking to my son. If you wanted to talk to me you should of called me like an adult instead of having my son call me to say what you wanted to say." He cut me off to say, "Why didn't you call me?" "I'm not finished talking. Don't cut me off. You are disrespecting me by telling my son to put me on speaker phone when I told him to take me off. I am not on your phone. I called Uncle Andre phone to talk to my son, not yours, so put my son on the phone." "Hello mommy." "Yea, you are going to come on back. Just because something look good does not mean it is, alright?" "Ok" "It's going to be alright. We know what the problem is. You just need to listen. So just listen, ok?" "Ok." "Okay, I will talk to you later, I love you." "I love you too, bye." I felt good about my decision because I knew that I made the best one. It made sense that Kareem would come back. Kareem was the answer, the connection, the bridge to my higher self. To love myself was to love him. And I knew that sending him away was running from myself. I made sense of it until I fell asleep. I had to be to work in a couple of hours. A text message came through from my uncle. I didn't open it. I rolled over instead, I had a sense that Uncle Rick's ego was bruised. I could tell that he had a big one. I knew that he wanted Kareem because he was lonely. He thought that Kareem was going to listen to him. But Kareem didn't and he switched on him. He punished him for a week for eating his pickle. Even though Kareem went to the store and bought him another one. He was just like me, my mother, grandma, all of us who could only deal with good kids. He must have thought I was lying about Kareem. He should have listened to me and then decide if he wanted to deal with that. But no, he thought he was special. He thought that he was so dope that Kareem would respect him even though he didn't respect his own mother. When I got up to get ready for my graveyard shift, I had opened my text. It read: You burn my sister picture fuck you I'm so glad you did what you did bye don't ever call me and your son told me that as well. I had knots in my stomach as I read it. This dude emotions were all over the place. And I had felt so peaceful. I wanted him to leave me alone already. He was immature and emotional. Why is he fucking with me? Who the fuck is he to question me about what I did with my picture? I wanted to say, "Yea mother fucker I burned a picture of my mother, and I will burn one of your mother too., if its mines. It would have been real, but he was too stupid to get it. He didn't even know that I did it for a good reason with his dum ass. I had started a bonfire in my backyard on a full moon. My kids and I and Uncle Andre joined a circle. We called in my mother, Daddy Leroy, grandma and grandpa and asked them to assist us in breaking the no love curse. I put a blown-up picture of my mom hugging Daddy Leroy. When I placed the picture on the fire, it burned through their hearts first. Everyone seen it. I stood there calling in the spirits asking them to show us the way to love, may we be love, to have the courage to love ourselves and everyone around us. After we all hugged each other and said I love you. I wasn't going to explain that to Uncle Rick. But I did text him back.

I am learning a lot about you…I hope that somewhere in your religion or somewhere that you learn to control your emotions…I will not explain anything to you because you deserve no explanation…but I will say this…disrespect me again and I will make the decision to stoop to your level and I will make you cry…I would say that I love you but I'm learning that it is just a word that people throw around and have no real meaning of the action behind it…so goodnight! I mean that sincerely, while I try to have a goodnight myself. Uncle Rick called my phone as soon as he got the text. I didn't answer. I knew he just wanted to argue. Who has time for that? He left me a message. "Why you not answering your phone, since you gonna make me cry. Answer the phone." I shook my head. He wanted to go back and forth with me. I decided to text him again. I texted: Why wont I answer the phone? Because there is nothing to talk about… didn't you say don't call your phone again…Well, I think that is best…we both got it established what we are doing, so enough said…I don't like talking to you, you talk over me, you have control issues, you just want to prove a point, your comprehension is not up to par, you lack understanding and talk to satisfy your emotions, not for a understanding or resolution…I am not miserable enough to play with you… and you just said fuck me I definitely don't want to talk to you. This is the last response you will get from me… you know why, because I don't care… no sleep lost. I got to go walk the fish now… GOODNIGHT. Uncle Rick kept calling me. I didn't answer. He kept texting me trying to get me to feed him with my energy. I never responded back. When Uncle Andre brought Kareem back home, he said that Uncle Rick said that he would mail my five hundred dollars to me. I couldn't stop laughing. But I never mentioned it.

CHAPTER 7

Judgement

When we cannot control our emotions, we judge people, and who are we to judge? Our lives were chosen at the time of incarnation. Let people do their part and have compassion for them, while they are doing it. We are all playing a role in this matrix. We are Spiritual Beings having a human experience. Everyone's experience doesn't have to be like yours. Even if someone hurts you, be grateful. They have done their job. Open your heart, open your mind. Hold your head up in power like a God and Goddess. Stop acting stupid, get serious and get loving. I'm telling you

Judgement

to love everyone because that's the only way to master your emotions.

People make me laugh. I was listening to this man talk. He kept talking about his niece working at taco bell. He was dissing her. He said that she needed to get a real job. Meanwhile his daughter didn't have a job at all.

I strongly suggest that you go to MyAstroData.com and seek out your moon sign. You will find this in your natal chart. You will find your natal chart on the site MyAstroData.com. You will have to plug in your information such as birthday, year and time of birth. Your natal chart will pop up. What that is, is a snapshot of the sky when you were born. That's how the planets were aligned and positioned in those houses. These planets take on meanings. This is why you are the way you are. This is who you are. This chart will tell you everything you need to know about you. People we need to know who we are. An astrologist such as myself can interpret this chart for you. Or you can learn. At the very least I want you to go find that little symbol of the moon. Where is it placed on your chart? Your moon sign is your emotional expression. In other words, how you express yourself. How you react in an emotional way and how you give your energy away. The way you share it. It is the part of you that fluctuates the most. This is because the moon is one of the fastest moving planets. The moon changes in every two and a half days. The phases are consistently changing. Your moon sign depicts how impulsive and how nurturing you are. For example, I have a Scorpio moon. How I know? Because my moon is sitting in the sign of Scorpio. You know what Scorpio's are like right? Ok! I am sensitive, loyal. I am very deep when it comes to how I feel. My emotions don't waiver, they are in fact intense. I can be jealous with my lover, overprotective and possessive. I can be mysterious and controlling. Full of sexuality and deeply passionate. Only my loved ones know the depth of my feelings behind my mysterious look. Yes, I am secretive. I suspect shit and this is where my questioning come from. This protects my sensitive parts. Keep in mind

Judgement

that the moon reflects characteristics that need to be changed. So, when you are trying to figure out why are you feeling the way you do and why you react the way you do. Just know that your moon sign plays a major part, and you should know it. When you are aware, it puts you in position to keep yourself in check, what do you like and don't like. Remember, you get to choose. You just have to be aware first. It will help you master your whole self.

You probably noticed that I have cussed quite a bit. But no, I don't have a potty mouth. It's just that, all the words in this book are placed exactly where they are supposed to be. And no, you don't have to be perfect to master emotions. It's all about strategy. It's about choosing in a world of duality. Be honest and up front about how you feel at all times.

You may have also noticed that I go back and forth writing in the past tense and the present all in the same sentence. I did this purposely. I am saying it how I want to say it. I like words but have never been crazy about the English language. I find it to be very manipulative. Like a lie. I am more concerned about what my soul is saying, and the spirit will channel it in a way it will reach the people it needs to.

Afterword

Let me say this. This book wont reach everyone. For some people this will be nothing more than a planted seed. You must be ready. You have to be tired. You must want more. I know some people who get this information for free. I drill it in them, freestyle. I could read this book to them, and it still won't make a difference. But guess what? That's ok. Some people won't get it in this lifetime but maybe the next. We all have a mission, a purpose to be here. You're not just here. You made an agreement with the cosmos's. We keep coming back here, each time mastering a little bit of it here and there, until we finally complete. I been here five times. Having a 3D experience for five thousand years. I am an old bird. This is my last time. I can't come back here again, and I don't want to, so I must get it this time. And guess what else? I know what I need to do. Somebody once asked, "How do you know?" What I told her was that everything is within us. All we have to do is remember. We are not here learning, we just become aware. What's my purpose? You're reading it. I have no choice but to embrace my pain. I was a hundred percent protected to make it back, to you.

He asked me who was I.

I am Queen Phoenix, incarnated on the yellow ray. The Goddess of beauty and wisdom. I am protected by a energy that you are not prepared to fuck with.

NAMASTE